WINGS, Wheels, and Keels

By Pat Miller-Schroeder

RSVP
RAINTREE
STECK-VAUGHN
PUBLISHERS

Published by Raintree Steck-Vaughn, an imprint of Steck-Vaughn Company

Library of Congress Cataloging-in-Publication Data

Miller-Schroeder, Patricia.
 Wings, wheels, and keels: the science of transportation /
 by Pat Miller-Schroeder.
  p. cm. — (Science@work)
 Includes bibliographical references.
 Summary: Describes different modes of transportation on the ground, in the air, and in the sea, and explains the scientific laws that affect them and allow them to work.
 ISBN 0-7398-0139-2
 1. Transportation—Juvenile literature. [1. Transportation.]
I. Title. II. Series: Science [at] work (Austin, Tex.)
TA1149.M55 2000
629.04—dc21   99-26889
               CIP

Printed and bound in Canada
1 2 3 4 5 6 7 8 9 0 04 03 02 01 00

Project Coordinator
Rennay Craats
Content Validator
Lois Edwards
Design
Warren Clark
Copy Editors
Meaghan Craven
Ann Sullivan
Kathy DeVico
Layout and Illustration
Chantelle Sales

Photograph Credits
Every reasonable effort has been made to trace ownership and to obtain permission to reprint copyright material. The publishers would be pleased to have any errors or omissions brought to their attention so that they may be corrected in subsequent printings.

Alberta Community Development, Reynolds-Alberta Museum: page 9; **Ballard Power Systems:** page 14; **Corel Corporation:** cover, pages 3, 4 (center), 5 (top left, top right, bottom left), 6, 7, 8, 10, 13, 16, 17, 18, 19, 21, 22, 27, 28, 30, 32 (bottom), 36, 38, 39, 42, 43, 45 (top left, top center, bottom right); **City of Calgary:** page 41; **Cu-Nim Gliding Club:** page 29; **Fisheries and Oceans Canada:** page 25; **Defence Canada:** pages 24, 35 (Rod Cando); **Detroit Public Library:** pages 11, 12; **Eyewire Incorporated:** cover, pages 2–3, 45 (top right), 44–48; ©1999 **Greenpeace/(Marjenburgh):** page 23; **NAV Canada:** pages 5, 33, 34; **Photodisc, Inc.:** pages 20, 40; **Softride:** page 4 (top); **USA Defense Visual Information Center:** page 37; **Maritime Museum, Vancouver, B.C.:** pages 26, 45 (bottom left); **The Vintage Locomotive Society Inc., Prairie Dog Central** page 15 (D. Shores).

Contents

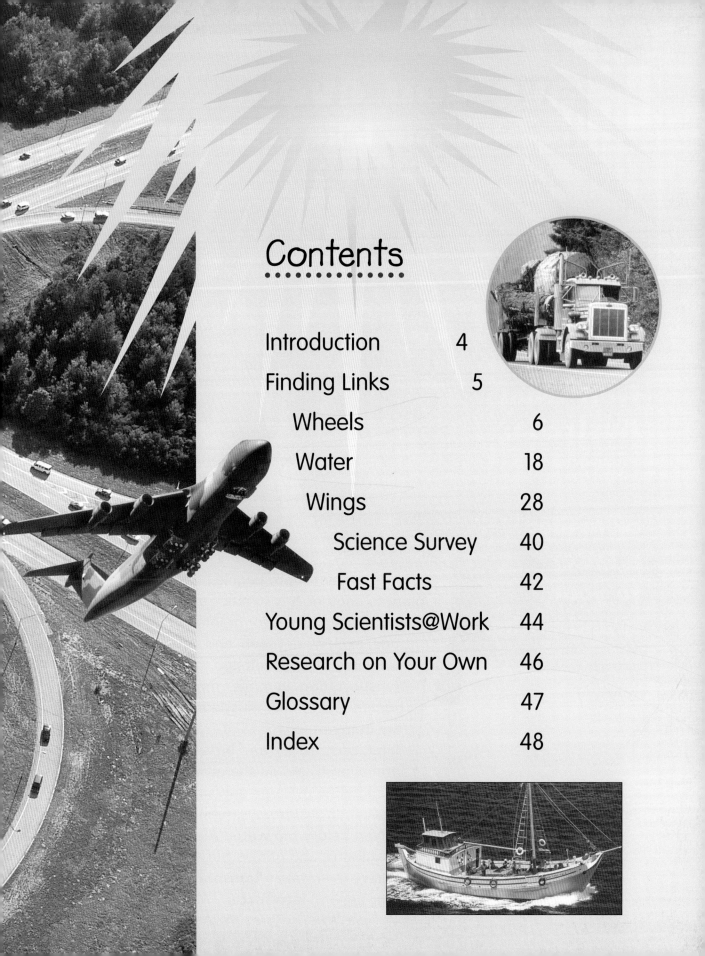

Have you ever pedaled your bike to school,

eaten kiwi fruit from Australia,

or mailed a letter to your grandmother?

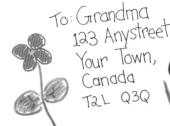

Jane Smith
200 Main Street
Anywhere, Canada
T15 050

To: Grandma
123 Anystreet
Your Town,
Canada
T2L Q3Q

If so, you have experienced three of the many ways transportation affects your life every day. Transportation is the moving of people or goods from one place to another. It is so much a part of most people's lives that they take it for granted. It helps us to visit, trade, explore, get food, and have fun.

People have developed many forms of transportation. In earlier times we relied on human and animal muscle power. Today there are many other forms of transportation. On land, cars, trucks, and buses fill the roads. Trains travel on tracks on the ground as well as above and below it. Large and small boats and ships travel on waterways, while submarines dive deep below the water. Airplanes, helicopters, balloons, and gliders busily fill the sky. We have even taken transportation to the Moon and far beyond into space.

FINDING LINKS

Society

Your community is affected by transportation. Businesses depend on trucks, planes, trains, and ships to get their products. People depend on cars, bicycles, and buses to get to work or school, or to visit family and friends across town or across the world.

The Environment

Sometimes the transportation that people use affects the environment in harmful ways. Burning fuel to power millions of cars around the world causes problems with air pollution and **global warming**. Millions of miles of roads and train tracks have changed natural habitats.

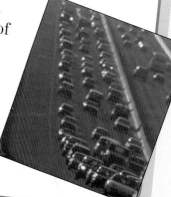

Technology

Transportation is so important to people that they are always looking for ways to improve it. Technology has allowed people to travel ever greater distances at faster speeds. It has given them ways to leave the land and travel on water, in the sky, and far into outer space.

Careers

There are many exciting careers to choose from in transportation. You could design or test new cars, or work as an air traffic controller at an airport. Any career you choose will likely be affected by transportation in some way.

Wheels

"Now we're rolling along!"

Can you imagine what life would be like without the wheel? Many things we depend on to make our lives easier and more fun would not exist. There would be no cars, trucks, trains, buses, bicycles, wagons, skateboards, or in-line skates. The world would be a slower place.

The first wheels were solid disks, probably cut from logs. Although they made moving loads easier, they were heavy and slow. About 4,000 years ago, lighter, spoked wheels gave chariot drivers a speed of about 20 miles per hour (32 kph). Today, trucks and trains move many tons of freight, and race cars and electric trains reach speeds of more than 200 miles per hour (320 kph).

Why use animal power?

The earliest form of transportation involved human muscle power. People traveled on foot, and anything they wanted to move had to be pushed, pulled, or carried. This limited how far they could go and how much they could take with them.

Things changed when people started to domesticate, or tame, animals. People controlled and used these animals for things such as meat, milk, wool, or work. Some animals helped with transportation. Dogs have been living with humans for at least 10,000 years. At first they helped with hunting and guarding, but later they carried packs and pulled loads on sleds. Sled dogs are still used today in some areas of the Far North.

Horses were the most important animal in transportation. Big, strong, and fast, horses could pull heavy loads and carry riders farther and faster than ever before. Horses worked on farms, in towns and cities, in mines, and with armies.

In Africa and the Middle East, camels have been important in transportation. For centuries, people have used these "ships of the desert" to cross the desert in caravans. Other animals used in transportation include donkeys, oxen, water buffalo, yaks, llamas, and elephants.

Some farmers still rely on the strength of oxen to help them do the heavy work involved in growing crops.

BYTE-SIZED FACT

Since horses were used for heavy jobs such as plowing, their strength became a unit of measurement. Today, engines are measured in a unit called horsepower. It is based on the pulling power of one working horse.

How do you balance on two wheels?

When learning to ride a bicycle, you have to learn to balance yourself on the bike. Forward movement keeps you from falling off the bike. You will also have better balance at higher speeds. That is because a bicycle wheel is a good example of a **gyroscope**. A gyroscope is a spinning wheel and axle held in a frame. When the wheel is spinning fast, it is hard to change the direction of its spin. Because of this, the gyroscope will not fall over. In the same way, your bicycle stays upright when you keep the wheels spinning by pedaling.

Going faster is easier to do with the sleek bicycles we have today than it was with earlier models.

Bicycles powered by human riders became common by the late 1700s. The first ones came in many shapes and sizes. Some had more than one seat. Others had wheels so large that the rider's feet could not touch the ground. Many early bicycles were unstable and unsafe. As materials and designs improved, bicycles became more popular.

When automobiles became common, many bicycle owners left their bikes for cars. Today bicycles are regaining their popularity. They provide cheap, pollution-free travel as well as good exercise and fun. In some countries, they are the main form of transportation. In China alone there are about one billion bicycles.

BYTE-SIZED FACT

The first motorcycle was invented in 1869. It was fueled by a tiny steam engine. Today gasoline engines and sleek shapes allow motorcycles to reach speeds of 150 miles per hour (240 kph).

Many cities have developed special bicycle paths to accommodate the growing number of people riding bicycles.

What were the first cars like?

The first automobiles looked very different from those on the road today. The first car sold to the public was made in Germany in 1885. It looked like a horseless carriage on three wheels. The car had no roof and was completely open to wind and rain. It had hand brakes and big, spoked bicycle wheels. In many of the first cars, both the front and back seats faced inward. The driver sat in the back seat and peered over the heads of those in the front seat.

The invention of the **internal combustion engine** in 1860 led to the rapid development of automobiles. These engines burned fuel, usually gasoline, inside a cylinder. A cylinder is a hollow metal tube with circular walls. A piston, which is a cylinder-shaped plug, moves snugly up and down inside the cylinder. An internal combustion engine works in four steps. First, the piston moves down the cylinder and sucks in a mixture of gas and air. The piston then moves up and compresses, or squeezes, the mixture. A spark sets the mixture burning. The gases expand and push the piston down. The piston moves back up and pushes the burned gases out of the engine.

Early cars had one or two large cylinders. An engine with only one cylinder has a jerky movement. The more cylinders in an automobile, the smoother the ride. Today's cars have four or more cylinders. They have a smoother ride and 40 times as much power as the first cars.

BYTE-SIZED FACT

Have you ever heard of a "red alert?" Early cars were considered dangerous. A man was supposed to walk in front of the car with a red flag to warn people to get out of the way.

By today's standards, the first cars were slow and hard to stop. Because the cars were open, drivers usually wore goggles and protective clothing.

Cars and Pollution

Automobiles are one of the most popular inventions humans have ever made.

At first only rich people could afford cars. That changed when Henry Ford began to mass-produce them in his Detroit factory in 1914. His Model T cars were all alike, painted black and low in price. By 1930, 15 million cars had been sold. Now there are more than 140 million cars in the United States and 14 million in Canada. Cars are one of the greatest threats to our environment.

Car engines release harmful gases into the atmosphere when they burn gasoline. These gases, called **emissions**, cause air pollution. They include carbon dioxide, nitrous oxide, and hydrocarbons. The average car gives off more than its own weight in carbon dioxide each year.

Modern cars are also faster than early cars. Driving fast causes more pollution than driving slowly for an equal distance. Driving 60 miles per hour (100 kph) burns 10 percent more gasoline than driving at 54 miles per hour (90 kph). Driving at 66 miles per hour (110 kph) burns 20 percent more gasoline.

The more gasoline burned, the more harmful emissions are released. This makes our air harmful to breathe and adds to the problem of global warming. Global warming is a worldwide warming trend that is made worse by certain gases.

BYTE-SIZED FACT
Three-fourths of the pollutants that combine to form smog in cities come from cars and other vehicles.

Emissions from the cars that people drive every day add to environmental problems, such as air pollution.

How are cars made?

At first, cars were made one at a time by small teams of workers. When Henry Ford started mass-producing cars, he changed that. In the Ford factory, cars were made on a moving assembly line. Workers assembled only one part of the car as it moved past them. Other workers farther down the line installed additional parts. This allowed more cars to be made cheaply. Most cars are still made this way today, but some assembly line workers have been replaced by robots.

In a car factory, there is usually one main assembly line and several smaller lines. Each of these lines puts together a different part of the car. The sides, roof, back, and floor are stamped out of metal or plastic and pressed into shape. These panels are then welded together to make the body shell. When the body shell is assembled and painted, it is moved to another line, where other parts are added. When the car rolls off the last line, it is tested to be sure all its parts work properly.

Each person working on a car assembly line contributes to the finished product.

Some factories specialize in certain car parts, not whole cars. At the Micro Compact Car (MCC) plant in France, cars are mass-produced among seven different factories. Each factory has an assembly line that specializes in a different car part. One entire car can be assembled in four hours.

BYTE-SIZED FACT

LINK TO   Careers

Car Designer

Henry Ford once said his customers could have any color they wanted on their Model Ts, his first mass-produced car, as long as it was black.

Today there are dozens of car styles, shapes, and colors to choose from. Car designers are constantly thinking of ways to make cars cheaper, safer, less polluting, and more attractive.

Most people who design cars work as part of a team. Team members may be trained in engineering, chemistry, physics, or computer science, or they may have other skills. They are usually employed by car manufacturers such as Ford, General Motors, or Toyota.

Designing a car requires many stages. Sketches of the new car design are made. Life-size clay models of the car are built. Computer-generated images of the design are created and analyzed. Next a model, or **prototype**, of the new car is built.

Once the prototype is built, it must be tested for safety and durability. In order to find any flaws, the car may be frozen and thawed, drenched with water, heated and cooled, shaken, twisted, and crashed. Car manufacturers and governments spend millions of dollars each year performing these tests. Special crash-test dummies are put in the car when it is crashed. The crash is filmed in slow motion to see what happens to the car and to the dummies inside. These tests have helped in the design of safety devices including shatter-proof windshields, seat belts, and air bags. The prototype is also tested for comfort and fuel use.

Crash-test dummies are used to test the safety of new cars.

BYTE-SIZED FACT

Air bags are safety features in many new cars. Hidden in the steering wheel or dashboard, they inflate in a fraction of a second if the car crashes.

Which vehicles handle the tough jobs?

Trucks are truly the workhorses of modern transportation. Bigger and stronger than cars, trucks come in many shapes and sizes to do tough jobs. Armored trucks move money to and from banks. Specially equipped trucks are used to fight fires. Monster trucks are used to entertain people by performing stunts of strength. Trucks pull loads of every description, such as food, lumber, cattle, furniture, stereos, and garbage. Trucks can deliver goods door to door. Even goods sent by boat or train often spend the first or last part of their trip on a truck.

Big semitrailer trucks have two parts. The tractor is the front part where the driver sits. The trailer is the part of the truck that carries the load. The tractor's job is to pull the load in the trailer attached behind it. Tractors can hook onto different sizes and shapes of trailers. This means that one tractor can pull many different kinds of loads. Truck tractors often have slopes on their roofs. These are air deflectors that make their trucks **streamlined**. Being streamlined means they have a smooth shape that lets air flow around and over them. This helps to save fuel when driving.

Truck drivers who travel long distances can pull off the road and sleep in their tractors. Some truck cabs have a special area behind the seat with bunks for sleeping. Some tractor cabs even have television sets, refrigerators, and stoves.

Semitrailer trucks provide an efficient way to haul logs and other loads.

Some of the biggest trucks in the world pull goods across the desert in Australia. They are called road trains, because one tractor pulls a row of several trailers.

BYTE-SIZED FACT

New Fuels

Researchers are looking for new ways to power cars. Most cars are powered by gasoline, which is a fossil fuel.

Fossil fuels, including gasoline, coal, and oil, are made from the remains of plants and animals that died millions of years ago. These fuels release harmful carbon monoxide into the air when burned. Researchers want to find ways that do not use up fossil fuels or pollute the environment. Two promising new methods are electric batteries and hydrogen **fuel cells**.

The idea of running a car on electricity stored in a battery is not new. The first electric car was built in 1839. Several hundred electric cars were built in the late 19th and early

20th centuries. Their main drawback then and now is that they can only go short distances before their batteries need to be recharged. Still, they are clean and quiet, and they produce no harmful emissions. A General Motors electric car can travel 160 miles (260 km) before needing to be recharged.

The hydrogen fuel cell is a device in which hydrogen combines with oxygen to make electricity. Hydrogen reacts with oxygen to form water, not harmful gases. The main drawback with hydrogen is that it is very flammable and difficult to store safely. Currently, researchers obtain

hydrogen from methanol (wood alcohol), which is safer to store. The car's fuel tank is filled with methanol. Methanol is mixed with oxygen in the fuel cell. Electricity is generated and powers an electric motor to drive the car. A vehicle powered by methanol produces half as much carbon monoxide as do gas-powered vehicles.

These fuel cells are in use powering transit buses in Vancouver, Canada. Researchers are working to improve them and make them more affordable.

In 1998 the Chicago Transit Authority began using buses powered by hydrogen fuel-cell-powered buses in a demonstration program.

How do you tie a country together?

Both Canada and the United States are large countries with people spread over thousands of miles. A transportation link was needed to tie the different parts of each country together. People and goods needed a way to move across the country. Projects were started to lay railroad tracks from coast to coast in both countries. Work started at the Pacific and Atlantic coasts and moved toward the middle. It was a hard job, laying thousands of miles of track as straight as possible. Workers had to bridge rivers, put trestles over valleys, and cut tunnels through mountains. They built trestles, wooden or steel frameworks, over ravines and valleys. The work of hundreds of people and horses was needed before the railroads were built.

The trains that traveled on these tracks were pulled by steam-powered locomotives. They were large and noisy, and they belched black smoke. Many animals and people were frightened by the locomotives.

As the train moved along, a fireman shoveled coal into the firebox to be burned. The fire heated water in the boiler to produce steam. The steam moved pistons back and forth to turn the engine wheels as the locomotive chugged along, pulling a train behind it.

Steam engines are still used in India, China, Africa, South America, and other areas. Most countries now use **diesel**, a light oil used as fuel, to run their trains. Diesel engines are more powerful than steam locomotives.

BYTE-SIZED FACT

Plenty of energy was wasted in making steam to run locomotives. Only about 7 percent of the coal burned produced heat and steam to power the engine. The other 93 percent of the coal's energy was wasted in steam that billowed from the locomotive's smokestack.

A boiler system creates the steam needed to run a steam-powered locomotive.

How do you get somewhere fast?

It seems people want to travel faster and faster these days. One way of moving large numbers of people over long distances is by high-speed electric train. The Japanese developed the first high-speed electric railroad in 1964. Their trains reached a speed of 130 miles per hour (210 kph), which was a record for that time. The trains were called "bullet trains" because of their shape and speed. Faster trains have been built since then. The German ICE (Intercity Express) can travel at 214 miles per hour (345 kph). The Chunnel Train moves through a tunnel 150 feet (46 m) beneath the English Channel, linking England and France. It travels at 186 miles per hour (300 kph).

High-speed trains are expensive to build because they need special tracks with gentle curves. Special overhead wires provide electricity. Control centers are set up to warn drivers of any problems or delays along the tracks.

BYTE-SIZED FACT

Magnetic Levitation Trains (MAGLEVs) float on a magnetic field. Electromagnetic wire coils are attached to the bottom of the train. They push against electromagnetic coils buried in the track. The coils push each other apart. This supports the train's weight. Additional magnetic forces push and pull the train along the track. There are no wheels or moving parts on the system to wear out or make noise. The Japanese have built a MAGLEV prototype that travels at more than 300 miles per hour (483 kph).

Thousands of people in Japan take a "bullet train" to work every day.

Commuting to Work

People once walked or rode in wagons or on horses to get to work or school. As cities grew larger, this was harder to do. People had to travel longer distances. Some took their new automobiles. For many others, new forms of transportation were needed.

Buses and streetcars were developed to help people move around the cities. The first ones in the 19th century were pulled by horses. Now buses have gasoline or diesel engines and come in many shapes and sizes. Extra-long buses have been tried in some cities. These buses have a joint in the middle that lets them bend when they go around corners. There are also small shuttle buses for short trips and double-decker buses for sight-seeing. Some cities still use streetcars. They run on tracks and are powered by electricity from overhead power lines.

Another way of moving people in cities is in underground railroads called subways. There are also aboveground elevated railroads, or **monorails**, in some cities. The train cars either run on top of the rail or hang below it.

As more people live in the suburbs and commute to work, buses and subways often become very crowded. In Tokyo, Japan, the subway is so crowded during rush hour that "shovers" are hired to cram passengers into the train cars. People are looking for other ways to commute. Some people carpool, while others ride bicycles or live where they can walk to work.

BYTE-SIZED FACT
In developing countries, buses are sometimes made from used trucks or other vehicles. They often carry extra passengers, luggage, or even livestock on the roof.

Streetcars are still a popular mode of public transit in San Francisco, California.

Water

"Anchors aweigh!"

Nearly three-fourths of Earth's surface is covered by water. For thousands of years, people have used waterways to help them move from place to place.

The first boats were invented when people learned to hollow out logs. People also learned to bend strips of wood or to weave reeds to make frames. Some of these early boats were covered with the skins of animals such as cows or seals. Some of these early boats were long, while others were round, like bowls. Today huge ships carry thousands of people and tons of freight across the oceans. Speedy motorboats skim the waves at more than 150 miles per hour (240 kph). Submarines explore the secrets in the depths of the oceans. The invention of the boat has been as important to transportation as the invention of the wheel.

How did we harness the wind?

Since earliest times, people have looked for ways to make travel on water easier, faster, and safer. One of the earliest developments was to harness the power of the wind to push boats along. The first known picture of a sail is 8,000 years old. Sails made of cloth or skins were attached with rope to upright poles, or masts. Early sails were square, but many other sail shapes and designs were used later. The wind produces a force called **thrust** that pushes against the sails to move boats forward. People had to learn ways of keeping the sails at the correct angle to catch the wind. Of course, the wind had to blow, or the ships would not move far at all.

Sailing ships have been used to explore new lands, to trade, and to go to war for thousands of years. Today they are mostly used for fishing, recreation, and sports. Big, engine-powered ships have taken over most of the other jobs that were once done by sailing ships.

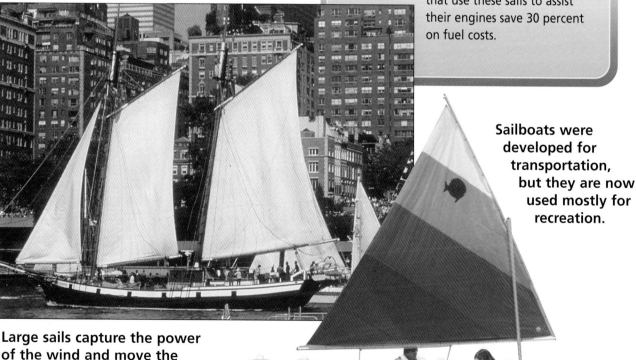

Sailboats were developed for transportation, but they are now used mostly for recreation.

Large sails capture the power of the wind and move the sailboat forward.

LINK TO [Technology]

Finding Your Way at Sea

There are no road signs or landmarks on the open ocean. One problem sailors have to solve is how to find their way at sea.

The first tool sailors used to help them find their way was the compass. A compass gives the direction of magnetic north. That direction can be used to tell which direction the ship is heading. Another tool sailors have used since 1730 is the sextant. Using a sextant, a sailor can measure the angle of the Sun or a star above the horizon. If he knows the time of day, he can calculate how far north or south of the equator he is.

Sailors also use special sea charts that show the routes used by other ships. Sea charts show where hidden dangers such as rocks or shipwrecks have been reported. All countries along seacoasts have lighthouses to warn ships that they are near land.

Modern ships are equipped with radios, **radar**, and computers. They can receive weather warnings or reports from coast guards or other ships. Computers on board

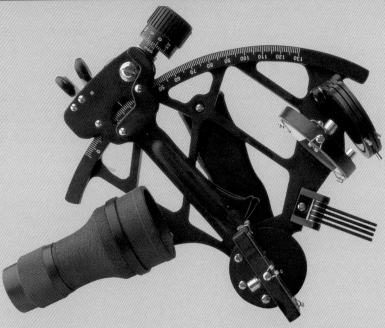

many ships are linked to radar. Radar is a device for showing the location of objects by bouncing radio waves off them and picking up echoes. This shows the speed, position, and direction in which nearby ships are traveling. It also warns of other hazards in a ship's path.

Hookups to satellite systems such as NAVSTAR can determine a ship's position anywhere in the world to within 300 feet (91 m). These systems can give the ship's

Early sailors relied on a sextant, shown above, to determine their position north or south of the equator.

exact latitude and longitude. Latitude is a measure of how far north or south of the equator a ship is. Longitude is a measure of how far east or west the ship is from the Prime Meridian, a specific location which passes through Greenwich, England.

BYTE-SIZED FACT

Most ships that weigh more than 300 tons have computerized autopilot systems. This allows the ship to navigate without its crew. In 1984 a Dutch freighter called *Pergo* was abandoned by its crew in stormy seas. Its computer autopilot sailed it safely for 200 miles (320 km) across the North Sea to Scotland with no one on board.

When is a boat a home?

The city of Venice, Italy, is connected by waterways called canals. Boats are an important mode of travel there.

Whole families live year-round on boats in many places. Houseboats are used in countries where land is scarce. On the island of Hong Kong, which is very crowded, the harbors are filled with houseboats. Small, flat-bottomed boats called junks are also used for fishing there. In the city of Amsterdam in the Netherlands, many "streets" are made of water. These watery streets, or **canals**, have houseboats rather than houses on them. In Venice, Italy, the whole city is linked by canals. Special water taxis called gondolas carry passengers on the canals. People travel to work and to school by boat rather than by car, and many people live on boats as well.

Most houseboats are flat-bottomed so they do not get stuck in shallow water. They are not usually equipped to handle rough seas.

> **BYTE-SIZED FACT**
>
> In rough seas boats pitch and roll. When a boat meets a wave head on, its bow moves up and down. This is called pitching. Waves from the side cause a side-to-side movement called rolling. Many boats have stabilizers, or special fins, on each side. These can be pushed out to keep the boat steady in rough water.

What followed wind power?

Sailing ships ruled the oceans for centuries. However, travel by sailing ships could be unreliable and slow. Even the fastest sailing ships clocked only 19 miles per hour (31 kph). By the early 1800s, steam engines were being used to turn paddle wheels and **propellers**. Today many ships are powered by diesel. The ship's engines turn one or more propellers at the back of the ship. These propellers can be enormous. They must also be very strong because the water they push is much heavier than air. The propellers produce a powerful thrust that pushes the ship forward and the water backward.

Engine-powered ships come in many shapes and sizes, depending on the jobs they do. Most big ships today are used to move cargo, or loads of goods, such as food, automobiles, or clothing. Trucks and trains bring cargo of all kinds to the docks. The cargo is usually packed in large square containers. These containers are lifted by crane onto the waiting ship. There is a big demand for ships that can carry loads of 1,000 tons or more.

Big, heavy ships cannot change course easily and can take several miles to stop. Small, powerful boats called tugboats are used to push and pull big ships in and out of harbors.

BYTE-SIZED FACT
What is the difference between a boat and a ship? You can put a boat on a ship, but you cannot put a ship on a boat.

How does a big ship stay afloat?

When a ship is put into water, it displaces, or pushes aside, some of the water. The water pushes back on the ship with a force equal to the weight of the displaced water. This allows the ship to float. As long as the force of the water pushing back is equal to or greater than the weight of the ship, the ship will stay afloat. Even if the ship carries a heavy load, it will not sink, as long as the shape of the ship displaces enough water.

Oil Spills

Nearly 75 percent of Earth is covered by water. Most of Earth's water lies in the oceans and seas. One of the worst forms of ocean pollution results from oil spills.

Many gigantic oil tankers carry oil across the oceans. These tankers can be more than 1,000 feet (300 m) long and carry 500,000 tons of oil. Such huge, heavy ships cannot change

BYTE-SIZED FACT

In 1989 the *Exxon Valdez* oil tanker ran aground in Prince William Sound in Alaska. It spilled more than 11 million gallons (42 million l) of oil that coated 1,500 miles (2,400 km) of coastline. The spill damaged national parks and wildlife refuges and killed unknown numbers of birds, fish, killer whales, seals, and sea otters. It destroyed the livelihood of local fishers. The Exxon company has paid more than $2 billion to clean up the oil, but pockets of pollution still remain.

course or stop quickly. Their crews have to be alert for ships or other hazards in their path. If an oil tanker sinks or collides with something, its cargo of oil will spill into the ocean. This causes terrible damage to the ocean environment and the plants and animals that live there. Many different kinds of fish, whales, seabirds, and seals have died in oil spills. The oil clings to them, making them sick. It can also poison their food source and habitat. When

Oil facilities are now trying to prepare for spills and clean-ups ahead of time, so they can deal with the damage quickly.

an oil spill occurs, it can cost billions of dollars to clean it up. The environment and sea creatures in the area may never recover.

The Coast Guard

Like many countries, Canada and the United States have ocean coastlines. An exciting career you may want to consider lies in the Canadian or American Coast Guard.

Men and women who work in the Coast Guard are highly trained and have an important job. They maintain the safety of ships and people on the waters off the Atlantic, Pacific, and Arctic coasts.

Coast Guard staff listen for distress signals from ships 24 hours a day, every day. They coordinate air and sea rescue missions for ships in trouble. They collect and broadcast weather reports and warnings. The Coast Guard monitors computer, radar, and satellite systems to provide up-to-date information on weather and hazards. Staff patrol the coastlines and offshore waters to prevent overfishing. They watch for and help clean up oil spills and other pollution.

BYTE-SIZED FACT

The Coast Guard's job is to help stop disasters like the sinking of the *Titanic*, which happened off the coast of Newfoundland in 1912. The *Titanic*, a huge ocean liner, was supposed to be unsinkable. On its first trip out, the ship struck an iceberg and sank. The *Titanic* did not have enough lifeboats for all its passengers. Of the 2,171 people aboard, 1,503 died in the icy Atlantic waters.

Coast Guard staff are often required to perform rescue missions at sea.

When is a boat not a boat?

The hovercraft looks like a fast boat skimming over the waves, but it is not really a boat. When its fans are off, the hovercraft sits on a flat, rubber skirt that rings the bottom of the craft. When the engine starts, air is blown in the hovercraft by large fans. The air is trapped by the rubber skirt long enough to support the hovercraft a few inches above the surface of the water. Propellers push the hovercraft forward. It can then travel at speeds of up to 78 mph (125 kph).

Hovercrafts can do something else that boats cannot do. They are **amphibious**, which means they can travel on land as well as on water. They can move from water to swamps, or fields, or even pavement.

A hydrofoil is a boat that skims the waves. It acts like an ordinary boat until it moves quickly. When the hydrofoil moves quickly, its front end is lifted out of the water on stilts called foils. Water moving past the foils generates **lift**. A propeller at the rear stays in the water and moves the boat. Hydrofoils can travel at speeds of up to 58 miles per hour (93 kph).

Make Your Own Hovercraft

1. Cut a circle, 4 to 5 inches (10 to 12 cm) in diameter, out of thick cardboard or plywood.

2. Make a small hole about 0.1 inches (2.5 mm) in the middle of the circle.

3. Glue a thread spool to the circle so that the hole in the spool lines up with the hole in the circle.

4. Cover the entire bottom end of the spool with glue so that air cannot leak out between the spool and the circle.

5. When the glue is dry, put the circle on a smooth, flat surface.

6. Inflate a balloon and twist the end so that the air cannot escape. Slip the end of the balloon over the top end of the spool.

7. Listen for the hiss of escaping air. Your hovercraft will be resting on a cushion of air.

8. Give the edge of your hovercraft a push. What happens? Try it over water. What happens?

Air trapped underneath the hovercraft supports the vehicle as it moves forward on land or on water.

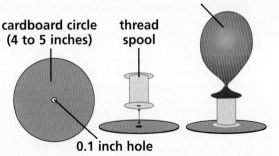

cardboard circle (4 to 5 inches)

thread spool

inflated balloon

0.1 inch hole

How can submarines stay underwater?

Traveling underwater poses special problems for humans. We have to carry our air with us so we can breathe. We also have to be protected from the pressure of the water above and around us, which could crush us.

Submarines are ships designed to meet these challenges. They have a double hull, or frame. Between the inner hull and the outer hull are areas that can be filled with seawater. This increases the submarine's weight and helps it to dive to great depths.

When it is time to head for the surface, the seawater can be pumped out to lighten the load. The submarine's inner hull is made of special steel that keeps it from being crushed by the enormous water pressure.

Once the submarine dives below the surface, its crew uses **sonar** to help it navigate. Sonar is a device that locates objects underwater by bouncing sound waves off them and measuring the echo.

When a submarine is just below the surface, the crew can use a periscope to see. This is a special viewing tube with glass and mirrors. It can be extended above the surface of the water while the submarine stays hidden below.

Modern nuclear submarines are equipped for up to two years underwater. They make their own fresh drinking water by distilling oceanwater. They also make their own supplies of air by freeing oxygen from freshwater.

Submarines come in many sizes. Large ones may be 560 feet (170 m) long and have a crew of 140 people. Small underwater crafts, called **submersibles**, may have a crew of two or three people. They may even be run by remote control from above the water. Submersibles are designed to work at depths of 1,500 feet (500 m) for short periods of time.

BYTE-SIZED FACT
Some whales use a system that is similar to sonar to help them navigate in the water.

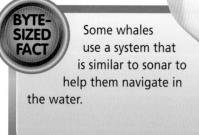

Small submersibles are useful for underwater research.

Harvesting the Sea

From earliest times, people have depended on boats to help them find food. The rivers, lakes, and oceans of the world provide many species of fish that people depend on.

People have also used boats to hunt whales and seals, and to trap shellfish such as crabs and lobsters. Many people fish from boats using hooks and lines. For bigger catches they use fishing boats with nets.

Whole schools, or large groups, of fish can be caught if nets are dragged on the surface and in the middle layers of water. The fish can then be hauled on board the ship or back to the beach. Other nets can be set in one place, where fish will swim into them and get tangled. Some fishing methods catch huge numbers of fish. Trawlers, which are fishing boats that use a large net, have been known to pull in 80 tons (72 tonnes) of herring in 20 minutes.

People used to think that the ocean's resources were limitless. We now know that some species of fish and whales are in danger of becoming extinct. We are now using ships to help us learn ways to use the ocean's resources wisely.

Trawlers catch fish in funnel-shaped nets that are dragged behind the boat.

Wings

"I want to soar with the eagles."

For thousands of years, people dreamed of flying like birds. In many cultures of the world, there are myths of heroes or gods who can fly. Many people tried to build wings of various sizes and shapes to take them into the sky. Some have even jumped off towers or cliffs wearing their homemade wings. None of these attempts at flight worked.

It took a lot of trial and error and knowledge of how birds really fly before people took their first flights. Orville and Wilbur Wright successfully flew the first engine-powered aircraft in 1903. Today airliners travel around the world at speeds of more than 600 miles per hour (965 kph), and people have flown to the Moon in spacecraft.

How did air travel begin?

The first successful air travel by humans began in balloons. For centuries, people have known that hot air rises because it is lighter than cold air. In 1783, two French brothers, Joseph and Etienne Montgolfier, developed a hot-air balloon. It was a huge linen bag lined with paper. Hot air to fuel it came from burning straw. The balloon's first passengers were a duck, a rooster, and a sheep. A few months later, the balloon carried two human passengers 5.6 miles (9 km) across Paris, France. At last humans could fly above Earth, but they could not yet control flight.

One type of air travel that is closer to the flight of birds is gliding. Gliders are aircraft with long wings and no motor that soar through the air on warm air currents called thermals. Thermals, or updrafts, rise from the sun-warmed ground. The glider is pulled into the air by an engine-powered airplane, then carried upward by the thermal in a spiral pattern.

The first manned gliders were developed in Germany in the 1890s by Otto Lilienthal. He studied bird flight and used that knowledge in his experiments with gliding. Lilienthal

Depending on the wind and weather conditions, a glider may soar for hours.

made more than 2,000 flights in his gliders. Some flights were more than 1,000 feet (305 m) long. His experiments were brought to a close in 1896. He died when a glider he was flying was caught in a wind gust and crashed.

Here is your challenge:

The wandering albatross is a seabird with a wingspan of 11 feet (3.3 m). Its long wings allow it to glide for miles over the open sea. Measure 11 feet (3.3 m) on the floor of your classroom to see how long this bird's wings are.

What are propeller-driven aircraft like?

In 1903 American brothers Orville and Wilbur Wright attached two propellers and a small gasoline engine to a glider type of plane. On its third flight, this first engine-powered aircraft stayed in the air 59 seconds and flew 852 feet (260 m). It was the first time people could control an airplane's takeoff and landing.

It was not long before propeller-driven airplanes were flying far greater distances. On June 14, 1919, Captain John Alcock and Lt. Arthur Brown made the first nonstop transatlantic flight aboard a World War I twin engine plane. These early pilots had to be tough. The **cockpits** of their planes were open to freezing rain and cold. Pilots had to wear protective clothing, including leather coats, gloves, boots, and helmets.

There are now many bigger and faster planes. However, small, propeller-driven planes are still used for many jobs. They can access places where bigger planes cannot land. Small planes need only a short runway, and they can use a field or roadway for takeoff and landing. They can be fitted with skis or pontoons, which are floats that support the airplane, to land on snow or water. These small planes serve as rescue craft and delivery vehicles, taking mail and supplies to remote places.

BYTE-SIZED FACT

Propeller-driven planes are used to fight forest fires. The Canadair-CL 415 can skim the surface of lakes, scooping up water into tanks. They can scoop up as much as 1,600 gallons (6,057 l) of water in 10 seconds. They then release their load of water over the forest fire.

Airplane propellers such as those on the Boeing B17 Bomber, have two or more blades, each of them shaped like an airplane wing.

How do we fly where we want?

There are four forces at work when a plane flies. **Drag** and **gravity** keep the plane back. Thrust and lift work to overcome the other two. Airplanes have several devices to help them work with these forces to fly. Propellers provide the thrust. They are made from two or more twisted blades. The engine causes the propeller's blades to rotate. The air is pushed out behind the blades, and the plane is pulled forward.

An airplane's wings, like a bird's wings, have a special shape to aid in flying. Their top is curved, and their bottom is nearly flat. The whole wing is tilted slightly so that it cuts through the air as the plane flies. During flight, the air pressure above the wing is lower than the air pressure underneath it. The difference in pressure gives the wing its lift.

Controlling the lift of airplanes is made easier by movable flaps on the wings and tail. These flaps are controlled by the pilot. They change the plane's lift for takeoff and landing.

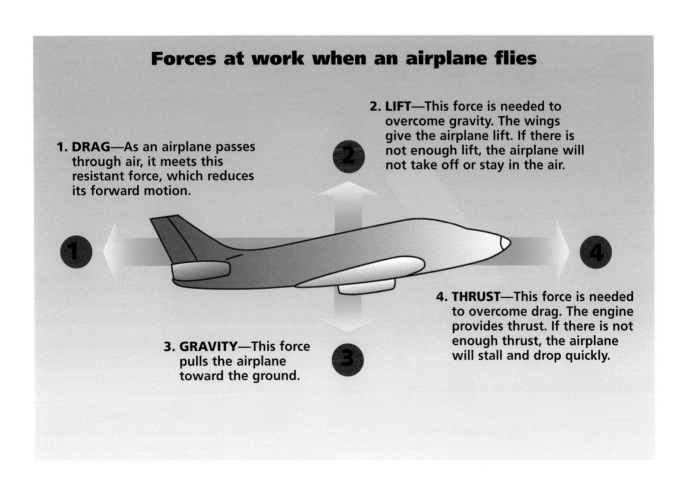

Forces at work when an airplane flies

1. DRAG—As an airplane passes through air, it meets this resistant force, which reduces its forward motion.

2. LIFT—This force is needed to overcome gravity. The wings give the airplane lift. If there is not enough lift, the airplane will not take off or stay in the air.

3. GRAVITY—This force pulls the airplane toward the ground.

4. THRUST—This force is needed to overcome drag. The engine provides thrust. If there is not enough thrust, the airplane will stall and drop quickly.

How big can airplanes get?

Today huge airplanes powered by jet engines carry passengers thousands of miles around the world. Among the largest of these airplanes are Boeing 747 jumbo jets. These giants are nearly as long as a football field and have a wingspan of 195 feet (60 m). They can carry 500 passengers comfortably on long trips of more than 12 hours. They cruise the sky at 600 miles per hour (965 kph).

Jumbo jets are powered by four powerful jet engines. These jet engines work by pushing the plane through the air. Fans at the front of the engine draw in air. About 20 percent of the air is then packed very tightly, or compressed, before it is mixed with fuel and burned. Hot gases escape from the engine in a powerful stream, or "jet." This, combined with air from the fan, gives the airliner the powerful thrust it needs to overcome the drag of the air on its heavy frame and load.

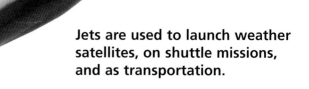

Jets are used to launch weather satellites, on shuttle missions, and as transportation.

Use a Balloon Model to See How a Jet Engine Works

Blow up a balloon, and twist the end shut. Release the end of the balloon. As the gas escapes, the balloon is thrust forward and flies through the air.

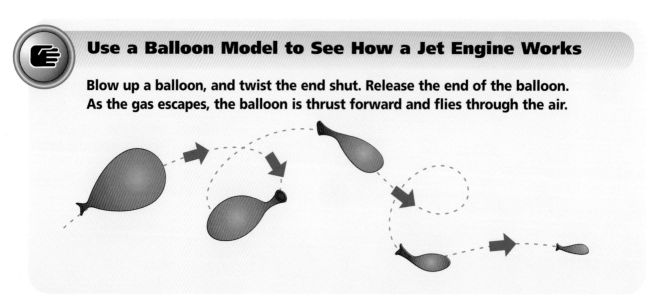

Air Traffic Controller

Large international airports are very busy places. Planes may be landing every 60 seconds. Other planes will be lined up in holding areas, waiting for their turn to take off. Air traffic controllers have the important job of making sure the planes arrive and depart safely with no collisions.

Local air traffic is directed from the control tower. Some controllers direct the movement of the planes on the ground. These might be planes that have already landed, planes that are moving into waiting lines, or planes that are being fueled and loaded.

Other controllers are in charge of directing the planes on the runways. They check radar screens to see the movements of planes that are arriving or have just taken off. Planes show up as blips of light on the radar screens. The location of all the planes around the airport can be seen. The controllers must keep a close watch on the planes' speed and direction of travel. They give directions and orders to the pilots by radio. Air traffic controllers have to be careful, alert, and cool in case of an emergency.

O'Hare International Airport in Chicago is the busiest airport in the world. It handles more than 4.5 million passengers every year. More than 2,000 airplanes land or take off daily from this airport.

BYTE-SIZED FACT

Air traffic controllers use the latest electronic equipment to ensure that airplanes take off and land safely.

Noise Pollution

Air travel is an increasingly popular way to travel. However, as airplanes get bigger and faster, there is growing concern about the noise they make.

Many airports are located close to heavily populated areas. The planes fly over homes and schools. Flights go many times during each day and often at night.

Negative effects from airplane noise have been reported in many places. Both people and animals have been affected. In Munich, Germany, schoolchildren living near a new airport developed health problems such as high blood pressure. They also showed high levels of stress. Another study showed that children living near an airport in New York were poor listeners and readers compared to children living in quieter areas. In Japan, it was reported that dairy cattle stopped giving milk near an air force base with low-flying planes. Aboriginal people from the northern part of Canada have reported that low-flying planes from a nearby military base made their children sick and frightened away the animals they hunted.

As airports expand and planes fly at greater speeds, people will have to find solutions to the problem of noise pollution.

Some airports use noise monitors to measure the sound made by airplanes taking off and landing.

BYTE-SIZED FACT
The fastest commercial airplane in the world is the Concorde, which has a cruising speed of 1,335 miles per hour (2,150 kph). This is twice the speed of sound, so it is called **supersonic**.

Search and Rescue

When people travel by land, water, or air, they sometimes have accidents or lose their way. People may have to be rescued from natural disasters such as floods, hurricanes, or earthquakes.

Often the best way to carry out a search and rescue mission is by air. Small planes can fly low and get into remote and hard-to-reach places. Their pilots often know the area they are searching well. The disadvantage of using small planes is that they may not have room to carry out several victims or bring in supplies. They also must land before they can pick anyone up. There may not be many places to land near a disaster site.

Another aircraft used for rescue work is the helicopter. Helicopters have large rotor blades mounted on top of the aircraft. These blades are turned by the engine and lift the helicopter straight up into the air. They also allow the helicopter to hover, or hang suspended in the air, in one spot. This is a big advantage.

Because they can hover, helicopters do not have to land to pick up people. A rescuer can be lowered to those needing help. Victims can be airlifted into the helicopter with a harness. A rescue helicopter carries medical equipment to treat people as soon as they are rescued. A helicopter can search for about four hours before having to refuel.

BYTE-SIZED FACT

Large helium-filled airships, or blimps, may be the rescue aircraft of the future. These safe, lighter-than-air airships can search for up to 55 hours at a time. They can carry heavy loads and remain in one spot. This makes them well suited to natural disaster rescue work.

Helicopters are useful in search and rescue missions in areas where it is impossible for airplanes to land.

What happens when you cross a helicopter with an airplane?

Aircraft designers are now combining the best features of airplanes and helicopters. New types of aircraft can now take off vertically and hover, as well as fly at high speeds. The *X-Wing Craft* looks like a space-age helicopter. Its body is streamlined like that of a fighter plane. An X-shaped helicopter **rotor unit** is mounted on top of the plane. This rotates while the plane takes off vertically or hovers. When the plane flies, the rotor blades lock in place and function as wings. The *X-Wing Craft* can reach speeds of 530 miles per hour (850 kph). Computers monitor the wings' position to help the pilot fly the aircraft.

Another craft that combines the features of helicopters and airplanes is the *Tilt-Rotor Craft*. During flight the engines stay in the normal position. However, when the *Tilt-Rotor* descends or takes off, the engines are tilted upward. The propellers then blow air directly downward like a helicopter.

Designs for some new aircraft combine features from helicopters and airplanes.

The maximum speed of an ordinary helicopter is about 200 miles per hour (320 kph). Higher speeds than this can damage rotor blades.

BYTE-SIZED FACT

Are there other types of new planes?

Today there are many special kinds of airplanes. Some of these planes can do things that sound like science fiction. Many modern fighter planes cannot be flown without the help of computers.

The *Harrier* is a special type of jet plane. It can act like a helicopter one minute and a supersonic jet the next. It is designed for quick vertical rises on takeoff. Its jet nozzles point downward to push the *Harrier* straight up. When the jet nozzles turn, the aircraft is pushed forward as well as up. Once the *Harrier* is at the proper speed, the jet nozzles turn fully back. Now the aircraft uses its full power to move forward. It can reach a top speed of 730 miles per hour (1,175 kph).

Swing Wing Planes can change their shape in flight. When these planes fly at low speeds, their wings are spread out. At high speeds the wings swing back for a more streamlined shape. All of these planes are military fighters or bombers.

A *Harrier II* jet can rise vertically on takeoff, the same way a helicopter does, and fly forward, as an airplane does.

> **BYTE-SIZED FACT**
>
> Space planes that will take passengers into orbit are being developed. They will take off and land from regular airport runways. However, they will fly into space at speeds of 18,600 miles per hour (30,000 kph). They will cross half the globe in 2 hours.

Traveling into Space

The 20th century has been a remarkable time for human transportation. In less than a century, human transportation has moved from the horse and buggy to space travel. Our top speed has gone from about 20 miles per hour (32 kph) to 25,000 miles per hour (40,230 kph).

Once humans had built supersonic airplanes, it seemed only a small step to space travel. However, taking transportation into space has required huge steps in technology. Spacecraft have to reach a speed of 25,000 miles per hour (40,230 kph) to escape the pull of gravity. Powerful booster rocket engines are needed to give enough thrust to reach this speed.

It takes only a few minutes for the spacecraft with its rocket booster engines to reach space. The rocket booster engines fall away, but the spacecraft carries on at the same speed. There is no drag to slow it down as it orbits Earth at a height of about 174 miles (280 km).

American space shuttles have made several trips into space. They carry astronauts and equipment for scientific experiments. Shuttles can link up with other spacecraft, such as they did with the Russian space station *Mir* and the *International Space Station*.

Space shuttles can stay in space for up to one month. When it is time to return, the shuttle must slow down to get out of Earth's orbit. It re-enters Earth's atmosphere nose first. Heat shields on the bottom and nose tip protect the shuttle and its crew from heat caused by air **friction**. The heat shields glow red hot as the shuttle encounters temperatures of up to 2,300°F (1,260°C) during re-entry. Parachutes help to slow the shuttle. Once it has slowed down, the shuttle glides to a landing like a big airplane.

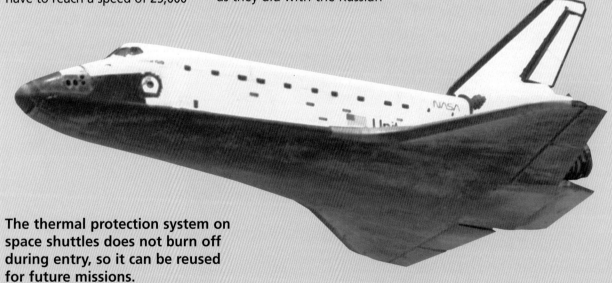

The thermal protection system on space shuttles does not burn off during entry, so it can be reused for future missions.

POINTS OF VIEW

Should the Government Spend Money to Explore Space?

For thousands of years, humans have traveled and explored every corner of the world. We are now taking our passion for discovery beyond Earth. Humans have walked on the Moon, and they have walked in space. We have sent unpiloted probes and robots to other planets, such as Mars, Venus, and Jupiter. We expect that someday humans will follow.

Our latest project is building the *International Space Station*. This incredible project involves help from the United States, Canada, Russia, Japan, Great Britain, and several other nations. This is the largest and most ambitious space project ever attempted. It will also be very expensive, costing billions of dollars to build and maintain. Construction is expected to be completed by 2004.

"This is a wonderful opportunity for people from different nations to work together. This project will bring good to all people of the world. It will add to world peace and security." **Astronaut involved with the project**

"How dare the politicians spend all that money on space travel when people are starving on Earth. That money should be used to provide homes and food for poor people." **Single mother of two living in a shelter for the homeless**

"The experiments that have been done in space and that will continue on the space station have already helped people on Earth. They have led to advances in medicine. Who knows what benefits the future will bring." **Doctor who treats heart patients helped by technology developed in the space program**

"Our government has other priorities we should focus on. We need to fight crime and lower our country's debt. Space travel is a nice idea but we have problems on Earth to solve first." **United States politician**

Do you think the government should spend money on space exploration?

Science Survey

There are many important questions we can consider about transportation. Cars, bicycles, rollerblades, and even our feet help us get around, but all of these forms of transportation can be dangerous. Some of the most important questions you can ask about transportation have to do with safety. You should consider what is safe for you and what is safe for your environment.

Answer these questions true or false

1. You only need to wear a bicycle helmet if you are riding in traffic.

2. The safest place for a child to sit is in the front seat of the car.

3. When you ride in a boat, it is safe to keep your life jacket where you can see it.

4. It is safe to walk on a train track after a train has passed by.

5. If you wear a bright color like red at night, you will be visible to traffic.

All answers are false.

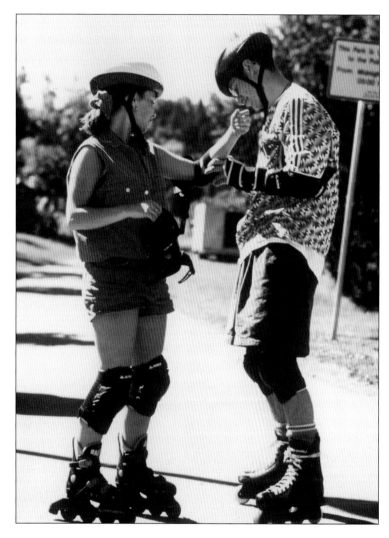

Here is your challenge:

Make a list of ten things you or your family could do to use transportation more responsibly.

Here are some suggestions:

1. **Walk to school or work.**

2. **Carpool.**

3. **Use a single trip in the car to run more than one errand.**

4. **Try out an alternative fuel source.**

5. **Ride the bus.**

6. **Do not throw garbage overboard when boating.**

Fast Facts

1. The maximum speed for Model T cars was 20 miles per hour (32 kph). This was the same speed as a team of fast horses.

2. A jet-powered car, Thrust SSC, driven by Andy Green of Britain, was the first land vehicle to break the sound barrier. The car reached a speed of 763 miles per hour (1,228 kph) in 1997.

3. Camel caravans, or groups traveling together in file, called the "Fast Ships of the Desert," average about 2.5 miles per hour (4 kph).

4. In 1930 Amy Johnson flew her Gypsy Moth airplane from England to Australia in 20 days. In 1989 a Boeing 747 jet with Qantas Airlines made the trip in 20 hours.

5. The world's longest freight train is in South Africa. It has 660 cars and is 4 miles (6.4 km) long.

6. Many semitrailer trucks are fitted with "under run guards" on their front and rear fenders. These keep cars from running underneath the truck in an accident.

7. The 100-mile (160-km) Suez Canal, which joins the Mediterranean Sea and the Red Sea, was built in 1869. Before then, boats had to sail thousands of miles around Africa to get from Europe to the Far East.

8. London, England, has the world's longest subway, with 253 miles (405 km) of track.

9. The first steam engine trains were slower than horses. In 1825 a steam engine in England was clocked at 4 miles per hour (6.4 kph).

10. Race cars are shaped so that air flowing over them keeps them on the road. They have front and rear wings that are shaped to push the wheels firmly onto the road at high speeds.

11. Jet planes that take off from the deck of aircraft carriers get a big boost. They are often shot out of a catapult, a device that launches them with enough speed to become airborne before the runway ends.

12. In 1969, two U.S. astronauts walked on the Moon, 238,857 miles (384,403 km) from Earth.

13. The *International Space Station* will have 460 tons (414 tonnes) of structures, modules, equipment, and supplies and will be put into orbit by 2004.

14. Three out of four drowning victims were not wearing life jackets.

15. The world's first fuel-cell-powered bus was driven in Vancouver, Canada, in 1993. After the trip Canadian officials drank a cup of clean water from the emissions of its hydrogen fuel.

16. The longest completely straight stretch of railroad track in the world is in Australia. It is a 297-mile (478-km) section between Sydney and Perth.

17. In 1984 the first Magnetic Levitation Train (MAGLEV) to carry passengers in Great Britain traveled between the airport and the railroad station in Birmingham. The distance traveled was 2,000 feet (610 m).

18. Canadians travel in automobiles nearly 10 percent more than residents of other industrialized countries do.

19. The first subway in London, England, in 1863 used steam trains, but drivers could not see in the tunnels due to smoke.

20. Each year about 35 million new cars are made worldwide.

Young Scientists@Work

Test your transportation knowledge with these questions and activities. You can probably answer the questions using only the information in this book, your own experience, and your common sense.

FACT: To minimize drag and create a smooth air flow, the bodies of many birds, fish, aircraft, and boats are streamlined. They are rounded and tapered, or narrow at the nose and tail. When air hits a flat surface, more drag is created.

TEST: Take a piece of cardboard about 3 inches x 6 inches (7.6 x 15 cm). Move the 3-inch edge just above the surface of water in a tub. Repeat with the edge of the cardboard just beneath the surface of the water. What differences do you observe? Repeat the experiment, using the 6-inch edge of the cardboard.

PREDICT: Will there be more drag with the edges above the water or below the water? Will there be more drag with the wider edge or the narrower edge?

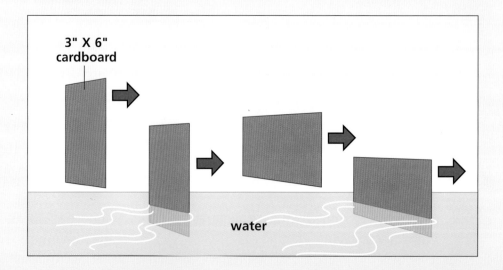

3" X 6" cardboard

water

FACT: Since earliest times humans have been looking for ways to improve transportation. One way we have measured improvement is by how fast or how far something goes.

TEST: Listed are five means of transportation. Match each one with the fastest speed it has reached.

1) team of horses
2) early steam locomotive
3) motorcycle
4) hovercraft
5) space shuttle

a) 20 mph (32 kph)
b) 150 mph (240 kph)
c) 78 mph (125 kph)
d) 25,000 mph (40,230 kph)
e) 4 mph (6.4 kph)

team of horses

steam locomotive

motorcycle

hovercraft

space shuttle

Answers: 1-a, 2-e, 3-b, 4-c, 5-d

Research on Your Own

There are many places to find out more about transportation. Your local library, museums, and the Internet all have excellent resources and information for you. Here are some great places to start.

Great Books

Davies, Eryl. *Transportation*. Toronto: Stoddart Publishing, 1995.

Galan, Mark, *Transportation: Understanding Science & Nature*. Alexandria, VA: Time Life Books, 1993.

Graham, Ian. *Aircraft*. Austin, TX: Raintree Steck-Vaughn, 1998.

Great Websites

CALSTART: Advanced Transportation Website
http://www.calstart.com/calindex3.html

Kennedy Space Center
http://www.ksc.nasa.gov/ksc.html

Mars Exploration Program
http://marsweb.jpl.nasa.gov/

National Air & Space Museum (How Things Fly)
http://www.nasm.edu/GALLERIES/GAL109/

NOVA Online Adventure: Deep-Sea Machines
http://www.pbs.org/wgbh/nova/abyss/frontier/deepsea.html

WebINK Auto Tour (So You Want to Make a Car...)
http://www.ipl.org/autou/

Glossary

amphibious: Able to travel on land and water

canal: Human-made waterway that is built for navigation

cockpit: The space near the front of an airplane that contains instruments, controls, and seats for the pilot and copilot

diesel: A type of light oil used as fuel in some engines

drag: The resistant force that holds a vehicle back

emissions: Gases or other products released into the atmosphere

friction: The force that opposes motion when two objects rub against each other

fuel cell: A device that produces electricity by a chemical reaction. There is no flame or pollution created.

global warming: Worldwide warming trend in climate that is made worse by the release of certain gases

gravity: The force that pulls objects toward Earth

gyroscope: A spinning wheel and axle held in a frame

internal combustion engine: Engine that burns fuel inside a cylinder

lift: The force needed to overcome gravity

monorail: Elevated train that rides on one rail

propeller: Two or more curved blades that spin around to make ships and planes move

prototype: The first one of its kind; the model used to test a design

radar: A device that locates objects by bouncing radio waves off them and measuring the echo

rotor unit: The rotating blades on top of a helicopter that help to lift it

sonar: A device that locates objects underwater by bouncing sound waves off them and measuring the echo

streamlined: Shaped to cut smoothly and quickly through air and water

submersible: Small craft designed to work underwater

supersonic: Faster than the speed of sound waves through air

thrust: The force that moves a vehicle forward

Index